T0062035

FRIEND REQUEST

INVENTION OF FACEBOOK AND INTERNET PRIVACY

Virginia Loh-Hagan

45TH PARALLEL PRESS

Published in the United States of America by Cherry Lake Publishing
Ann Arbor, Michigan
www.cherrylakepublishing.com

Reading Adviser: Beth Walker Gambro, MS, Ed., Reading Consultant, Yorkville, IL
Cover Designer: Felicia Macheske

Photo Credits: © Naruedom Yaempongsa/Shutterstock, cover, 1; © Frederic Legrand - COMEO/Shutterstock.com, 5, 17; © Ink Drop/Shutterstock.com, 6; © Heidi Bessen/Shutterstock.com, 11; © Andrey_Popov/Shutterstock.com, 12; © Jayson Photography/Shutterstock.com, 21; © Samuel Borges Photography/Shutterstock.com, 22; © sergey causelove/Shutterstock.com, 25; © blvdone/Shutterstock.com, 27

Graphic Elements Throughout: © Chipmunk 131/Shutterstock.com; © Nowik Sylwia/Shutterstock.com; © Andrey_Popov/Shutterstock.com; © NadzeyaShanchuk/Shutterstock.com; © KathyGold/Shutterstock.com; © Black creator/Shutterstock.com; © Edvard Molnar/Shutterstock.com; © Elenadesign/Shutterstock.com; © estherpoon/Shutterstock.com

45th Parallel Press is an imprint of Cherry Lake Publishing.

Library of Congress Cataloging-in-Publication Data
Names: Loh-Hagan, Virginia, author.
Title: Friend request : invention of Facebook and internet privacy / by Virginia Loh-Hagan.
Description: Ann Arbor, Michigan : Cherry Lake Publishing, 2022. | Series: Behind the curtain
Identifiers: LCCN 2021037477 | ISBN 9781534199460 (hardcover) | ISBN 9781668900604 (paperback) | ISBN 9781668902042 (pdf) | ISBN 9781668906361 (ebook)
Subjects: LCSH: Facebook (Firm)—Juvenile literature. | Social media—Juvenile literature. | Internet and children—Juvenile literature.
Classification: LCC HM743.F33 L64 2022 | DDC 302.23/1—dc23
LC record available at https://lccn.loc.gov/2021037477

Cherry Lake Publishing would like to acknowledge the work of the Partnership for 21st Century Learning, a Network of Battelle for Kids. Please visit *http://www.battelleforkids.org/networks/p21* for more information.

Printed in the United States of America
Corporate Graphics

A Note on Dramatic Retellings

Participating in Readers Theater, or dramatic retellings, can greatly improve reading skills, especially fluency. The books in the **BEHIND THE CURTAIN** series give readers opportunities to learn about important historical events in a fun and engaging way. These books serve as a bridge to more complex texts. All the characters and stories have been fictionalized. To learn more, check out the Perspectives Library series and the Modern Perspectives series, as **BEHIND THE CURTAIN** books are aligned to these stories.

TABLE of CONTENTS

HISTORICAL BACKGROUND

In 2004, Mark Zuckerberg was a college student. He studied at Harvard University in Massachusetts. He was good at computer coding. He wanted to connect with other college students. He launched Facebook. Facebook is a social media website. It became a hit. Today, it has nearly 3 billion users per month. It's used all around the world. It's the biggest social media network.

People create profiles. They share photos. They chat. They join groups. They share a lot of information. Facebook inspired more user-generated content on the web. People had more access to information. But this also causes issues with privacy. Facebook added more privacy controls.

FLASH FACT!

Mark Zuckerberg became the world's youngest billionaire. He pledged to donate half his wealth to good causes.

Vocabulary

coding (KOH-ding) the process of creating instructions for computers using programming languages

user-generated (YOO-suhr JEH-nuh-ray-tuhd) information on a website that is created by people

privacy (PRY-vuh-see) the state of being free from public attention

FLASH FACT!

Facebook, now called Meta Platforms, Inc., owns Instagram and WhatsApp.

Vocabulary
investors (in-VEH-stuhrz) people who put money into companies to make a profit

Before Facebook, Zuckerberg invented FaceMash. Harvard students voted between 2 women. They decided who was more attractive. FaceMash made people mad. Women's rights groups protested. Zuckerberg had to take it down. He violated many university rules. He violated people's privacy. FaceMash was not a good idea. But it was really popular. Zuckerberg realized the value of an online social network.

At first, Facebook was only for Harvard students. It spread. Other colleges used it. Soon, many more people used it. Zuckerberg got investors. Facebook became a big business. More social media networks were created. Today, people do most everything online. We are connected globally.

CAST of CHARACTERS

NARRATOR: person who helps tells the story

JON: a male student at Harvard University

HEATHER: a female student at Harvard University

DR. CONNORS: a **professor** at Harvard University

KARA: a female student at Harvard University

SPOTLIGHT
AMPLIFICATION OF AN ACTIVIST

Nguyen Ngoc Nhu Quynh blogs as "Mother Mushroom." She is from Vietnam. She's an activist who fights for human rights. At first, she blogged to trade parenting tips. Then she blogged to address social issues. In 2006, she visited a hospital in Vietnam. Poor people were ignored. They didn't have money to bribe officials to let them in. They died. Quynh thought this was unfair. She openly criticized the Vietnamese government. She said the government was violating human rights. She said the government was corrupt. She blogged about police brutality and free speech. She encouraged people to share thoughts on Facebook. She was first arrested in 2009. She kept fighting. She kept getting arrested. In 2018, she fled to the United States for safety.

Vocabulary
professor (pruh-FEH-suhr)
a teacher at the university level

FLASH FACT!

Facebook is the third most popular site in the world. Google and YouTube are the first and second most popular sites.

ACT 1

NARRATOR: *It's 2003.* **JON** *and* **HEATHER** *are students at Harvard University in Massachusetts. Jon and Heather are talking.*

JON: Did you sign up for FaceMash? Everyone's talking about it.

HEATHER: Why would I sign up for that? It's disrespectful to women. If you're my friend, you shouldn't sign up either.

JON: It's just for fun. I don't see the harm.

HEATHER: I don't see the fun. And I see a lot of harm.

JON: You're on it. People are saying you're hot. That's a **compliment**. You should feel good.

HEATHER: Nothing about that makes me feel good. Rating women on their looks is mean. It's also wrong. It sets women up as objects. We're people. We're not things.

JON: You're right. I didn't think about it that way.

Vocabulary
compliment (KAHM-pluh-muhnt)
praise or admiration

FLASH FACT!
#MeToo movement started in 2006. It's a movement abolishing violence against women. It started on MySpace. MySpace was a social network site before Facebook.

HEATHER: How would you like it if we rated men? What if we clicked whether you were hot or not?

JON: That wouldn't feel good.

HEATHER: Another issue is privacy. I didn't give permission to have my photos posted.

JON: That's a good point. Photos are personal. I don't know how I would feel about having my photos out there.

HEATHER: It makes me feel unsafe. I'm going to complain about that.

NARRATOR: *It's the next day. Heather is talking to* **DR. CONNORS,** *a Harvard professor. She is in Dr. Connors's office.*

HEATHER: Mark Zuckerberg's website is gross. It should be taken down.

DR. CONNORS: I agree with you. Zuckerberg has violated several university **policies**.

HEATHER: Like what?

DR. CONNORS: He **hacked** into our system. He **breached** our security.

Vocabulary

policies (PAH-luh-seez) a set of guidelines or rules

hacked (HAKD) broke into computer systems

breached (BREECHD) violated

FLASH FACT!

Cybercriminals hack into systems. They steal data. They hold it for ransom.

HEATHER: How is that possible? Shouldn't there be more protections?

DR. CONNORS: Internet security is always an issue. We do our best. We get smarter about it. But so do hackers. It's hard to keep up.

HEATHER: Will he get in trouble for violating privacy?

DR. CONNORS: Yes. He copied student photos. He used those photos for his website.

HEATHER: It feels like he stole our photos.

DR. CONNORS: He violated individual privacy. He violated **copyrights**. These are serious concerns.

HEATHER: When will FaceMash be taken down?

DR. CONNORS: It should already be down. It was up for only two days.

SPOTLIGHT
A SPECIAL EFFECT

Today people can get famous on social media. Being an influencer is a real job. Influencers are online personalities. They have a lot of followers. They partner with companies to advertise their products. The average salary for an influencer is about $60,000 a year. The most popular social media sites for influencers are Instagram, TikTok, and YouTube. Charli D'Amelio is the most popular teen influencer on TikTok. She was the first to get more than 100 million followers. She was 16 years old at the time. She's a dancer and posted dance videos. In 2020, she earned more than $4 million. The biggest influencer in the world is Portuguese pro soccer player Cristiano Ronaldo. He has more than 500 million followers.

Vocabulary
copyrights (KAH-pee-rytes)
exclusive rights belonging to the owner
of intellectual property

FLASH FACT!

*The most popular topics
for influencers are fashion
and gaming.*

HEATHER: Damage was still done. At least 450 students visited the site. They voted more than 22,000 times. This is about more than just internet issues. It's **sexist**.

DR. CONNORS: It definitely set the women's rights movement back. We got several complaint letters from **campus** groups.

HEATHER: I have friends in Fuerza Latina and the Association of Black Harvard Women. These groups fight for women's rights. They sent letters.

DR. CONNORS: They're not the only ones who complained. Faculty and staff are upset too. This is not who we are. We don't treat people like this.

HEATHER: Have you talked to Zuckerberg yet?

DR. CONNORS: We reached out to him. He's aware of the concerns.

HEATHER: What did he have to say?

DR. CONNORS: He said he didn't mean to break rules. He said he didn't mean to hurt anyone.

Vocabulary

sexist (SEK-sist) showing prejudice or bias against women

campus (KAM-puhs) the grounds and buildings of a university or college

FLASH FACT!

Governments need to protect internet data. Cybersecurity laws are meant to protect users.

HEATHER: Then why did he do it?

DR. CONNORS: He's a coder. He was more interested in the idea. He liked the computer program.

HEATHER: Will the school punish him?

DR. CONNORS: There's a **hearing** next week. He'll have a chance to explain his side. We will be deciding whether or not to **expel** him.

HEATHER: I don't think he should be kicked out. But he should be better.

NARRATOR: *A couple of weeks have passed. Jon and Heather are talking.*

JON: Did you hear what happened to Zuckerberg?

HEATHER: Yes. Dr. Connors informed all who complained.

JON: What happened?

HEATHER: He was put on **probation**. He has to see a counselor. He has to send apology letters.

JON: How do you feel about that?

HEATHER: He has skills as a coder. I'm sure he'll invent more programs. But I hope he learns from this. Anything on the internet reaches so many people. We have to be responsible.

Vocabulary

hearing (HIHR-ing) a trial or an opportunity to state one's case

expel (ik-SPEHL) force to leave

probation (proh-BAY-shuhn) a period of time when someone is under supervision

FLASH FACT!

Facebook hosts Hackathon events. People come together. They come up with new ideas.

NARRATOR: *One year has passed. It's 2004.* **JON** *and* **HEATHER** *are still at Harvard. They're talking.*

JON: Zuckerberg did it again. He created another program.

HEATHER: I hope it's not a "hot or not" website. That would be messed up.

JON: It's not. It's called "The Facebook."

HEATHER: Like the student **directories**?

JON: Yes. Instead of on paper, the information is online. No more trees have to die!

HEATHER: I like the idea of saving paper. But what's the point of going online?

JON: It's like a big online social club. It's easier to connect. I like it a lot better.

HEATHER: That doesn't sound too bad.

JON: We can make friends more easily. We can connect with friends of our friends. We can meet people we probably wouldn't meet otherwise.

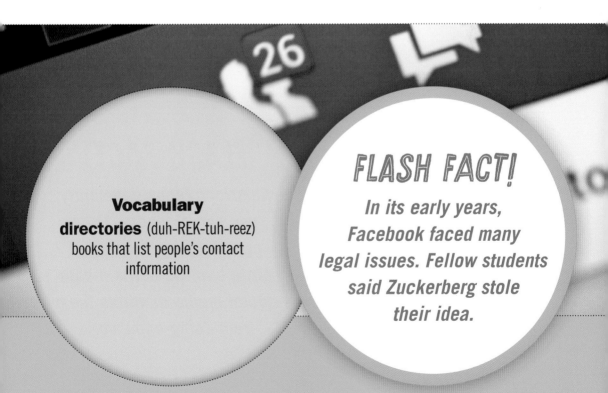

Vocabulary
directories (duh-REK-tuh-reez) books that list people's contact information

FLASH FACT!
In its early years, Facebook faced many legal issues. Fellow students said Zuckerberg stole their idea.

Vocabulary
distraction (dih-STRAK-shuhn)
a thing that prevents someone from
giving full attention to something else

FLASH FACT!

*American teens constantly
use social media. They
prefer texting to talking.
More than 50 percent said
social media distracts them
from doing homework.*

HEATHER: What else can you do?

JON: You can send messages. You can ask questions. It's fun.

HEATHER: I came here to study. I don't need the **distraction**.

JON: You can use The Facebook for school too.

HEATHER: How so?

JON: You can connect with people. You can set up study groups. I did that yesterday. It was so easy. I sent out a message. People messaged me back. We formed a study group. We set up a date and time.

HEATHER: Do you have it open on your computer? Can I see how it works?

NARRATOR: *Heather and Jon spend time looking at the website.*

HEATHER: That's a lot of information shared online. The website has photos. It lists birthdays. It lists addresses. It lists phone numbers.

JON: The paper directories list that information too. What's the difference?

HEATHER: Only people with paper directories can access information. But information feels less safe online. Anyone can access it. Information is harder to control online.

JON: Only people at Harvard have access to The Facebook.

Vocabulary
clamoring (KLA-muh-ring) making a demand
glimpses (GLIM-suhz) brief looks

FLASH FACT!

Today, anyone 13 years old or older can get a Facebook profile.

HEATHER: That's not going to last long. I bet other schools are **clamoring** for it.

NARRATOR: *It's 2 years later, in 2006. The Facebook is now just called Facebook. Facebook has also spread beyond Harvard. Jon and Heather are about to graduate.* **KARA** *is another student. Jon, Heather, and Kara are talking. They're on the Harvard campus.*

JON: You still don't have a profile on Facebook. We'll be graduating soon. I would love to stay connected.

HEATHER: You can always call or email me.

JON: It's easier to keep up on Facebook.

KARA: That's true. It's fun seeing **glimpses** of people's life. I've learned so much about people. Everyone is on it.

HEATHER: Not everyone. I don't plan on joining.

JON: Why not?

HEATHER: I don't feel comfortable putting my personal info online.

KARA: What are you afraid of?

HEATHER: Hackers could use my personal information. They steal identities. They steal bank accounts. They can do a lot of damage.

JON: You can change your privacy settings. You can block people.

HEATHER: Hackers will always find a way. They're 2 steps ahead of us.

JON: Zuckerberg is working on ways to protect privacy.

SPOTLIGHT

Facebook has a new policy. Famous people who incite unrest or violence will be suspended. This is to protect public safety. In 2020, President Donald Trump lost the presidential election. On January 6, 2021, a mob attacked the U.S. Capitol. The Capitol is the meeting place for Congress. There was a violent riot. Trump used social media a lot. He used it to encourage the rioters. Facebook shut off his account during the Capitol riots. It said Trump's actions were "a severe violation of rules." Facebook suspended Trump's Facebook and Instagram accounts for 2 years. Trump has also been banned from other social media platforms. He viewed these bans as an insult. He said, "They shouldn't be allowed to get away with this censoring and silencing..." Freedom of speech is a tough topic. It raises more questions than answers.

FLASH FACT!

Around 70 percent of Americans use Facebook. Women use it more than men.

HEATHER: How does Zuckerberg have time to do all this? I'm barely passing my classes.

KARA: Didn't you know? Zuckerberg dropped out of Harvard. He did only 2 years of college.

HEATHER: I hadn't heard. He must be doing well.

KARA: He's making tons of money. Investors are contacting him all the time.

JON: I heard he turned down an offer from Google.

HEATHER: Is he charging people to join Facebook? If so, I'm definitely not joining.

JON: It's free. That was really important to Zuckerberg. He didn't want to charge users. He wanted everyone to have access to it.

HEATHER: I don't understand. How does he make money?

KARA: He gets money from **advertisements**. Companies pay to promote themselves.

HEATHER: Why would companies pay Facebook?

KARA: Facebook has tons of users. Users see these advertisements. They may buy things from the companies. It's worth it to companies.

HEATHER: It's a brave new online world.

Vocabulary
advertisements
(ad-ver-TIZE-muhnts) notices promoting a product, service, or event

FLASH FACT!

Social media sites tailor ads to reflect people's interests. Some people see this as a violation of privacy.

FLASH FORWARD
CURRENT CONNECTIONS

Facebook was invented in 2004. Its legacy lives on. We feel its effects all the time. There is much for us to think about.

- **Use social media as activism:** The year 2020 was a busy one. There was the COVID-19 pandemic. There was racial unrest. There was an upcoming presidential election. The year 2020 saw a rise in activism. Some people marched in street protests. But COVID forced many people to stay home. This increased online activism. Users share information about protests and causes. They spread ideas. This is called slacktivism or clicktivism. It includes signing online petitions and sharing hashtags. Some people criticize online activism. They say it doesn't lead to change. They say it's fake and only for show. Other people think online activism is useful. It's important to start somewhere.

- **Be smart online:** There's a lot of information online. Some of it is true. Some of it is not. Fake news is misinformation. Some people have limited facts. They may try to mislead people. They may not do research. Some people think social media sites have a responsibility to stop the spread of misinformation. It's important to be critical. Check all the facts and the sources. Know the difference between facts and opinions.

- **Be safe online:** There are fake accounts on social media. Some people want to steal identities or even hurt others. Protect your privacy. Keep your devices updated so you have the latest security programs. Set strong passwords. Don't share passwords. Don't click on links you don't know or share personal information. It's important to protect yourself.

CONSIDER THIS!

TAKE A POSITION! Anonymity means not being known by name. Some people are active online. But they don't use their real names. Why do people do this? What are the pros and cons? Should people allowed to be anonymous? Argue your point with reasons and evidence.

SAY WHAT? Internet trolls are people who upset others online. They make rude comments. Learn more. Explain how to identify internet trolls. Explain how to deal with internet trolls.

THINK ABOUT IT! Think about your screen time. How much time do you spend on your cell phone? How much time do you spend watching TV? Reduce your screen time. Go outside. Do more active things. Why is too much screen time bad?

Learn More

Gitlin, Martin. *The Birth of Modern Tech*. Ann Arbor, MI: Cherry Lake Publishing, 2022.

Hudak, Heather C. *Cell Phone Privacy*. Minneapolis, MN: Abdo Publishing, 2019.

Loh-Hagan, Virginia. *Tech*. Ann Arbor, MI: Cherry Lake Publishing, 2021.

Orr, Tamra B. *Invention of Facebook and Internet Privacy*. Ann Arbor, MI: Cherry Lake Publishing, 2017.

INDEX

ABOUT THE AUTHOR

Dr. Virginia Loh-Hagan is an author, former K–8 teacher, curriculum designer, and university professor. She's currently the director of the Asian Pacific Islander Desi American (APIDA) Center at San Diego State University. She started using email and social media in college. She can't remember what life was like before that. She lives in San Diego with her one very tall husband and two very naughty dogs.